Charles Desmarais Gardette

The Fire-Fiend

And other poems

Charles Desmarais Gardette

The Fire-Fiend
And other poems

ISBN/EAN: 9783337256654

Printed in Europe, USA, Canada, Australia, Japan

Cover: Foto ©Thomas Meinert / pixelio.de

More available books at **www.hansebooks.com**

THE FIRE-FIEND,

AND

Other Poems.

BY

CHARLES D. GARDETTE.

NEW YORK:

BUNCE AND HUNTINGTON, PUBLISHERS.

M.DCCC.LXVI.

PRE·NOTE.

———

A FEW—and but a few—words of explanation seem appropriate here, with reference to the poem which gives title to this volume.

The "FIRE-FIEND" was written some six years ago, in consequence of a literary discussion wherein it was asserted, that the marked originality of style, both as to conception and expression, in the poems of the late EDGAR ALLEN POE, rendered a successful imitation difficult even to impossibility. The author was challenged to produce a poem, in the manner of "*The Raven*," which should be accepted by the general critic as a genuine composition of Mr. POE's, and the "FIRE-FIEND" was the result.

This poem was printed as "from an unpublished MS. of the late EDGAR A. POE," and the hoax proved sufficiently successful to deceive a number of critics in this country, and also in England where it was afterward republished (by Mr. MACREADY, the tragedian), in the *London Star*, as an undoubted production of its *soi-disant* author.

The comments upon it, by the various critics, professional and other, who accepted it as Mr. POE'S, were too flattering to be quoted here, the more especially, since, had the poem appeared simply as the composition of its real author, these gentlemen would probably have been slow to discover in it the same merits.

The true history of the poem and its actual authorship being thus succinctly given, there seems nothing further to be said, than to remain, very respectfully, the Reader's humble servant,

THE AUTHOR.

CONTENTS.

THE FIRE-FIEND:

A NIGHTMARE.

I.

IN the deepest dearth of Midnight, while the sad and
    solemn swell
Still was floating, faintly echoed from the Forest Chapel
    Bell—
Faintly, falteringly floating o'er the sable waves of air
That were through the Midnight rolling, chafed and bil-
    lowy with the tolling—
In my chamber I lay dreaming by the fire-light's fitful
    gleaming,
And my dreams were dreams foreshadowed on a heart
    foredoomed to Care!

II.

As the last long lingering echo of the Midnight's mystic
    chime—
Lifting through the sable billows to the Thither Shore
    of Time—

Leaving on the starless silence not a token nor a trace—

In a quivering sigh departed; from my couch in fear I
    started :

Started to my feet in terror, for my Dream's phantasmal
    Error

Painted in the fitful fire a frightful, fiendish, flaming face!

III.

On the red hearth's reddest centre, from a blazing knot
    of oak,

Seemed to gibe and grin this Phantom when in terror I
    awoke,

And my slumberous eyelids straining as I staggered to
    the floor,

Still in that dread Vision seeming, turned my gaze toward
    the gleaming

Hearth, and—there!—oh, God! I saw It! and from out
    Its flaming jaw It

Spat a ceaseless, seething, hissing, bubbling, gurgling
    stream of gore!

IV.

Speechless; struck with stony silence ; frozen to the floor
    I stood,

Till methought my brain was hissing with that hissing, bubbling blood :—

Till I felt my life-stream oozing, oozing from those lambent lips :—

Till the Demon seemed to name me :—then a wondrous calm o'ercame me,

And my brow grew cold and dewy, with a death-damp stiff and gluey,

And I fell back on my pillow in apparent soul-eclipse !

v.

Then, as in Death's seeming shadow, in the icy Pall of Fear

I lay stricken, came a hoarse and hideous murmur to my ear :—

Came a murmur like the murmur of assassins in their sleep :—

Muttering, "Higher ! higher ! higher ! I am Demon of the Fire !

I am Arch-Fiend of the Fire ! and each blazing roof's my pyre,

And my sweetest incense is the blood and tears my victims weep !"

1*

VI.

" How I revel on the Prairie! How I roar among the
    Pines!

How I laugh when from the village o'er the snow the
    red flame shines,

And I hear the shrieks of terror, with a Life in every
    breath!

How I scream with lambent laughter as I hurl each
    crackling rafter

Down the fell abyss of Fire, until higher! higher! higher!

Leap the High-Priests of my Altar in their merry Dance
    of Death!"

VII.

" I am Monarch of the Fire! I am Vassal-King of
    Death!

World-encircling, with the shadow of its Doom upon my
    breath!

With the symbol of Hereafter flaming from my fatal
    face!

I command the Eternal Fire! Higher! higher! higher!
    higher!

Leap my ministering Demons, like Phantasmagoric lemans

Hugging Universal Nature in their hideous embrace!"

VIII.

Then a sombre silence shut me in a solemn, shrouded
    sleep,

And I slumbered, like an infant in the "Cradle of the
    Deep,"

Till the Belfry in the Forest quivered with the matin
    stroke,

And the martins, from the edges of its lichen-lidded ledges,

Shimmered through the russet arches where the Light in
    torn files marches,

Like a routed army struggling through the serried ranks
    of oak.

IX.

Through my ivy-fretted casement filtered in a tremulous
    note

From the tall and stately linden where a Robin swelled
    his throat :—

Querulous, quaker-breasted Robin, calling quaintly for his
    mate !

Then I started up, unbidden, from my slumber Night-
    mare ridden,

With the memory of that Dire Demon in my central Fire

On my eye's interior mirror like the shadow of a Fate !

X.

Ah! the fiendish Fire had smouldered to a white and
formless heap,

And no knot of oak was flaming as it flamed upon my
sleep;

But around its very centre, where the Demon Face had
shone,

Forkèd Shadows seemed to linger, pointing as with spectral finger

To a BIBLE, massive, golden, on a table carved and
olden—

And I bowed, and said, "All Power is of God, of God
alone!"

GOLGOTHA:

A PHANTASM.

WHILE the embers flare and flicker, gathering
shadows thick and thicker—
While the slender, shaded lamplight sheds a glimmer gray
and dull—
On my mantel, smoke-incrusted, o'er two war-knives
hacked and rusted,
In my fascinated vision grins a dark and dented Skull!

Through the Midnight Forest leaping—Death's red har-
vest fresh from reaping—
Once this Skull was steeped and drunken in a revelry
of gore:
In his crimson orgie shrieking, mad with lust, and murder-
reeking—
Thus the Blood-Avenger found him—smote him!—and
he raved no more!

In that Forest, leaf-enfolded, many a nameless year he
mouldered,

Withered, shrivelled, fell to utter dry and desolate decay;

Till of all his savage glory naught there was to tell the
story

Save this dark uncouth and dented Skull I found, and
bore away!

With the coward thought to mock it, in each eyeball's
blackened socket

Once I set a globe of silver, as a dread and dismal jest.

Oh! full often has the glitter of those pale globes caused
a bitter

Burst of sharp and sudden terror to a timid twilight
guest!

But, to-night, their flashes daunt me, and their changing
glances haunt me,

And their cold glare shivers through me like a scymitar
of ice!

Well I know their threat is seeming—that no life is in
their gleaming,

Yet my soul is strangely troubled by my own accurst
device!

Ay! my soul is strangely troubled! And my heart-throbs
fiercely doubled!

And I cannot wrench my gaze from off those silver
    demon-balls !

To my brain their blaze seems burning—ah ! by Heaven !
    I saw them turning !

Yes ! see—see them ! there ! they roll ! O God ! a red
    light from them falls !

     *   *   *   *

How its white teeth glint and glisten ! Listen ! Am I
    mad ? O ! listen !

No ! It speaks ! I hear a whisper rattle through its hol-
    low jaws !—

" With this jest my front adorning, Pale-Face, you are
    blindly scorning,—

Sadly, sorrowfully scorning all your Being's Primal Laws !

" Count the dim descent of Ages ! Turn Life's crisp and
    crumbling pages !

Is a single Leaf forgotten in this Golgotha of Doom ?

Fool ! You bear a fragile, carnal shroud around your
    ghastly charnel,

But to add another atom to the Inevitable Loom !

" I have stripped my shroud before you : You, perchance,
    now wear it o'er you !

Every shred of Life is woven from the Dead Past, o'er
and o'er !

Through the Years the Earth is heaving with this weird
and wondrous weaving,

And your slender thread but waiteth till the Loom hath
need of more !"

   *   *   *   *

It hath ceased ! There is no glimmer on the hearth !
The lamp grows dimmer,

Dimmer, dimmer—now it flickers, flashes, wildly flares—
is fled !

Through the Darkness round me heaving, now I hear a
sound of weaving,

As a Mighty Loom were working, viewless, with a viewless thread !

WAR ECHOES.

PEACE, THE VICTIM.

NOON! and above the further hills
   There floats a sea of purple mist,
   Whose tremulous depth of amethyst
With amber sun-tide ebbs and fills.

Within yon slope of wooded deeps,
   Where in a shadowed glory nod
   The blossoms of the golden rod,
A slumber-laden South wind creeps.

Through tangled grasses, scarcely stirred,
   The loitering brook, with silent flow
   Slips toward the languid lake below,
Where knee-deep stand the listless herd.

The stirless draperies of the air
   Wrap me as in the sensuous folds
   Of an Arcadian dream, that holds
Its spell of Peace forever there.

Peace, dove-eyed Goddess! Lo! I kneel,
  Here at thy stainless shrine, and swear——
  Hark! 'tis the trumpet's angry blare!
And yonder gleams the glint of steel!

Fast through the purple mist they break:
  Their chargers thunder down the steep;
  And from the glamour of their sleep
The valley's thousand echoes wake.

The startled air in surges sweeps
  Athwart the lake: the herd is fled:
  The golden rod lies crushed and dead
Within 'the ravaged woodland deeps.

And Peace? Upon her sacred plain,
  Her altar with fraternal gore
  Smokes redly: by her Southern shore
Stalks Treason with the brand of Cain.

LINT.

FIBRE by fibre, shred by shred,
　　It falls from her delicate hand
In feathery films, as soft and slow
As fall the flakes of a vanishing snow
　　In the lap of a summer land.

There are jewels of price in her roseate ears,
　　And gold round her white wrist coils:
There are costly trifles on every hand,
And gems of art from many a land,
　　In the chamber where she toils.

A rare bird sings in a gilded cage
　　At the open casement near:
A sun-ray glints through a swaying bough,
And lights with a diamond radiance now
　　The dew of a falling tear!

A sob floats out to the summer air
　　With the song-bird's latest trill:

The gossamer folds of the drapery
Are waved by the swell of a long, low sigh,
 And the delicate hands are still.

"Ah! beauty of earth is naught, is naught!
 And a gilded youth is vain!
I have seen a sister's scarred face shine
With a youth and beauty all divine
 By the soldier's couch of pain!

" I have read of another, whose passing shade
 On their pillows, the mangled kissed,
In the far Crimea!"—There are no more tears;
But she plucks the gems from her delicate ears,
 And the gold from her slender wrist.

The bird still sings in his gilded cage;
 But the Angel in her heart
Hath stung her soul with a noble pain,
And beauty is naught, and youth is vain,
 While the Patriot's wounds still smart!
        *   *   *   *
Fibre by fibre, shred by shred,
 Still fall from her delicate hand

The feathery films, as soft and slow
As fall the flakes of a vanishing snow
   In the lap of a summer land.

There are crimson stains on breasts and brows,
   And fillets in ghastly coils :
The walls are lofty, and white, and bare,
And moaning echoes roll ever there
   Through the chamber where she toils.

No glitter of gold on her slender wrist,
   Nor gem in her roseate ears ;
But a youth and a beauty all divine
In the face of the Christian maiden shine,
   And her gems are the soldier's tears !

"AN UNCLAIMED BODY."

UNKNOWN, unclaimed, forgotten;
　　In a rude, unlettered bier;
With the death-wound on his fair young brow,
In a nameless grave he sleepeth now,
　　Unhallowed by a tear!
　　　*　　　*　　　*　　　*
Darkly the cloud of battle
　　Hangs o'er the Field of Pines:
With desperate might the rebels bear
Their famine-driven squadrons there,
　　Upon our slender lines.

The shadowy belts of forest
　　With ghastly flames are red:
By copse and bramble, plain and wood,
Lie, prone or writhing in their blood,
　　The dying and the dead.

Who is yon gallant stripling
　　Far in our battle's van,
Who combats as if Freedom's charm

Had nerved his heart and steeled his arm
  Beyond the might of man?

Within the deepest woodland,
  When faint the conflict grew—
His dress in deadly grapple shred,
Blackened his face, and bare his head—
  He fell!—and no one knew!
      *   *   *   *
Sweet are the song-birds' carols:
  The flowers of June are fair:
The stream laughs gaily in the sun;
But by its margin walketh one
  Who sees no laughter there.

Her slender form is drooping:
  Her dark-blue eye is dim:
The sun-rays nestle in her hair;
The birds still sing; the flowers are fair—
  She only thinks of *him!*

" Oh! that this mad rebellion
  By prayers and tears could cease;
And he—my golden thread of life—
Were here, unbroken, from the strife,
  To give my poor heart peace!

  2

" I love thee, oh, my country !
  I love thee from my soul !
My life I would not count a shade,
A feather, on thine altar laid,
  If it could make thee whole !

" But *his!* ah ! spare my other,
  My nobler, better part !
Thou still hast myriad hero souls
To shine on Glory's martyr-rolls ;
  But *he* is all my heart !"

The summer flowers still open,
  And the bee their honey sips ;
But alas ! for the weeping maiden there,
With the sunshine rippling o'er her hair,
  And the prayer on her trembling lips !

Unclaimed, unknown, forgotten ;
  In a rude, unlettered bier ;
With the death-wound on his fair young brow,
In a nameless grave *he* sleepeth now,
  Unhallowed by a tear !

THE TWO SOLDIERS.

I.

TWO maids walked by the shining sea;
  One with a crown of raven hair,
And one with her tresses flowing free,
  And the golden noon-rays nestling there.

" Heart of mine "—thus the dark maid cried—
  " None save a soldier shall e'er command !
With a soul of flame, and an eye of pride,
  And his gleaming sword in his good right hand !"

" Mine I give "—said the fair-haired maid—
  " Even as thou, to a soldier's care :
In the cause of Truth is his soul arrayed,
  With the sword of Faith and the shield of Prayer."

II.

Two youths walked by the forest green ;
  One with a haughty brow and eye,
And one with a calm and gentle mien
  That cheered the soul of the passer-by.

" Raven locks and an eye of jet;
   A proud lipp'd maid with a tropic cheek;
Such is the snare for my heart set!"
   Thus did the haughty Southron speak.

" Tresses of gold," his comrade said;
   " Eyes like the depths of a summer sea;
Cheeks where the bosom's truth is read;
   Such is the guileless heart for me!"

III.

Two by the shining sea once more:
   Tresses of gold, and raven hair:
And two in the shade of the forest hoar:
   The haughty brow, and the brow so fair.

Crispèd hands in the locks of jet:
   The proud lips clenched, and the dark eye sear;
But the tresses of gold in a sable net,
   And the blue eye bright with a chastening tear!

The fire quenched in the Southron eye:
   The dark brow prone on the rebel sod;
But the fair face turned to the summer sky,
   And the patriot soul at peace with God.

THE CRIPPLE AT THE GATE.

L OOK ! how the hoofs and wheels to-day
    Scatter the dust on the broad highway,
Where Beauty, and Fashion, and Wealth, and Pride,
On saddle and cushion serenely ride !
The very steeds have a conscious prance
   Of pride in their elegant freight !
Love and laughter like jewels slip
From the sparkling eye and the merry lip :
You never would think that the Nation's life
Hung on the thread of a desperate strife,
Unless from these you should turn, by chance,
   To the Cripple at the Gate.

Weary, and footsore, and ragged, and soiled,
Through the summer glare he has slowly toiled
Along the edge of the broad highway,
Since the early dawn of the westering day :
His rags are flecked with the dusky foam
   That flew from the gilded bits

Of the champing steeds that passed him by,
And a haggard shadow is in his eye;
But it is not the gloom of an envious pain!
He has left a limb on the battle-plain,
And, to win his way to his distant home,
    At my gate, a Beggar, he sits!

He tells me his tale in a simple way:
"I had nothing," he says, "except my pay,
And a wife and four little girls, and so
I sent all my money to them, you know!
When I lost my limb, Sir—but that I'm lame
    I do not complain, for, you see,
'Tis the fortune of war, and it might be worse;
And I'd lose the other to stop the curse
Of this terrible strife! But I meant to say,
When I left the hospital t'other day,
I *did* think I had a kind of a claim
    To be sent to my village free.

" Don't you think it hard yourself, Sir? True,
There's a hundred dollars of bounty due
In three years, or when the war's over; but how
Long may that be—can you tell me now?

I did not enlist for bounty, I trust;
  My conscience I never have sold;
But how does it look for a soldier to 'tramp,'
Begging his way like a vagabond scamp,
From the fields where he often risked his life,
To the home where he left his babes and wife,
In a uniform made of tatters and dust
  Instead of the 'blue and gold?'

"Whose fault this is, Sir, I do not know,"
Said the wayworn man as he rose to go;
"But of this, alas! I am sure—the sight
Of a soldier returning in such a plight
To the home whence, a few short months ago,
  He marched in a gallant band,
With music, and banners, and shining steel,
Will dull more ears to the battle-peal,
And cause more bosoms with doubt to swell,
Than the secret traitor's deadliest spell:
Don't you see yourself, Sir, it must be so?"
  And he sighed as I held out my hand.

Lofty carriage and low *coupe*
Still whirl the dust on the broad highway:

Beauty, and Fashion, and Wealth, and Pride,
Still through the roseate twilight ride,
With love, and laughter, and prancing steed,
　　As if Pleasure were all life's fate.
But I gaze no more on the joyous train,
For my eye is fixed with a steadfast strain
On the tattered soldier's halting stride,
Till his tall form sinks down the dark hill-side;
Then I cry, " Thank God! he hath *now* no need
　　To beg at the stranger's gate!"

THE NOONDAY STREET.

I WALKED the city's noonday street,
  Wrapt in a veil of idle thought,
That oft betrayed my careless feet
  To wander from the path I sought.

In silken rustlings, to and fro,
  The flock of Fashion fluttered there;
And woman's laugh, of silver flow,
  With fragrant ripples stirred the air.

The sun sheen glanced on gem and gold,
  Along the causeway's glittering side;
While o'er its echoing centre rolled
  Full many an equipage of pride.

I strayed, and knew not where I strayed;
  Till, sudden, on my heart a pain—
And on my path there fell a shade,—
  That rent my veil of thought in twain.
   2*

I looked, and lo ! the vision grew
　　To life !　I stood beneath an arch,
And saw them passing, two by two,
　　And heard the echoes of their march.

They bore two torn and blood-stained flags ;
　　No silken vesture, gold, nor gem :
Their battle-trophies and their rags
　　Were all the sun might gild for them !

Scarred, crippled, crutched, they onward pressed,
　　With music whose firm measure made
Their tottering step a bitter jest :
　　They passed !　Once more I onward strayed.

They passed : I loitered in their path :
　　They toiled the throngs of Fashion through :
Not one of those, methought, but hath
　　From all of these a life-debt due !

They passed : afar I followed them,
　　Walking the noonday street once more—
The laugh still rang ! on gold and gem
　　The sun still glittered as before !

THE BROKEN SWORD.

HER soul caught up Hope's shining shield
 Against the dark assaults of Doubt :
She bade him bravely to the field
 Where Death holds Glory's standard out.

She girt the good steel on his thigh,
 And, " Rumor's random shafts," she said,
" Full oft are poisoned with a lie
 That strikes the unwitting victim dead.

" If you—God give me strength !—should bleed,
 Yet stanch life's current ere it fail ;
Send me this scabbard ! I will heed
 No other token, tongue, nor tale !

" If captive ; in the rebel host
 Some youth, heart-mated, there must be
Who, for her sake or loved or lost,
 Will speed your ransomed blade to me.

"If—if—I cannot speak the word!
   Pray some true comrade—at the worst—
In pity hither bear the sword;
   But bid, oh! bid him break it first!"

Time sped.   And Rumor still forbore
   To strike her with its venomed dart:
Hope's buckler, still undimmed, she wore,
   A constant Ægis, on her heart!

Till—surely 'twas a love divine
   That armed her soul with daily prayer—
A soldier found her at the shrine,
   And laid a broken falchion there!

"You broke the blade at *his* command?"
   She faltered.   "Nay, true heart, not so!
Twas shivered, in his good right hand,
   Full on the forehead of his foe!"

"To the just cause I freely gave
   My better life," she said, and pressed
To her pale lips the shattered glaive:
   "To God I dedicate the rest!

"Yet is my mission here to do!
　I hear *his* stricken brethren groan:
Many their pangs, their soothers few;—
　Be they my heralds to the Throne!"

Self-vowed, to wounds and death she bears
　Her Master's healing and His word;
But ever at her side she wears,
　For rosary, the broken sword!

THE THREE WATCHERS.

WISTFULLY through the sunshine,
    Wistfully through the rain,
They watch for his returning
    Who will never return again.

Three little cherub faces,
    Close to the window pane,
Wistfully watching and waiting
    For him who returns not again.

Frigidly under the sunbeams,
    Frigidly under the storm,
Where the battle dead are thickest,
    Lies a pallid and pulseless form.

Sign, nor mark, nor token
    To tell of the hero's name;
But clasped to his gory bosom
    Is a fragile picture-frame.

A simple, poor medallion,
  Death-clutched with a wisp of grass ;
But three little cherub faces
  Smile through the blood-stained glass.

Rude are the hands that lay him
  On the soldier's humble pall ;
Yet tears from the bearded faces
  On the cherub faces fall.

The grasp of the Dead hath stiffened
  Round the picture on his breast,
And they leave those faces smiling
  On the nameless soldier's rest.

    *   *   *   *

Then there came a voice, like an echo,
  Through the sunshine and the rain :
" Look up ! for on earth, your father
  Shall never return again !"

And the eldest, looking upward,
  " Our Father in heaven," she said,
" Thou hast taken our other father,
  Let us come to Thee instead !"

"SISTERS OF MERCY."

AWAY! dissectors of God's Word,
Who think that Heaven its path directs
By guide-posts, with the cant of sects
Whose writings, all save yours, are blurred!

What are your glimmering rushlights worth
Amid the radiance all divine
That makes these humble Sisters shine
Like angels ministering on earth?

If ye would learn how Heaven is won,
Go where your stricken brethren lie
In long, pale ranks of agony,
And see how Mercy's work is done!

List, where the wounded soldier sleeps,
The name, that, potent as a prayer,
Sighed through the lips of anguish there,
Like balm o'er all his senses creeps!

Seek those dread chambers, if ye dare,
 Where lurks in every passing breath
 Contagion, with his brother Death,
And reverence Mercy's mission there!

There is no peril, pain, nor toil,
 No wounds, no pestilence, no despair,
 But finds some white-coifed Sister there
To pour the sacred wine and oil!

Know, ye who prate of "form" and "law,"
 That one Samaritan in deed
 May sanctify the faultiest creed,
While you are grappling with a straw!

AT THE OUTPOST.

"THERE is no moon, but the night is clear—
　　Clear and cold, and the stars are few.
In the shadow of Death I am walking here:
　　In the shadow of Death, at twenty-two!

"A year ago, on a night like this—
　　One brief year!—from a maid I knew,
In the shadow of Love I asked a kiss:
　　In the shadow of Love she gave me two.

"Two, and a third, and another yet—
　　One more yet, and she whispered, 'Go!
On the hazard of strife my love I set:
　　On the hazard of strife, for weal or woe!'

"'My country first!' Oh, the peerless maid!
　　Not her peer hath the maid I know!
'My country first,' in that kiss she said:
　　'My country first!' and she bade me go.

" Say you a drink ?   Good comrade, no !
    Ah ! the love of a maid like mine
Flushes the heart with a godlike glow :
    Flushes the heart like Olympian wine !

" A cypher of gold with a braid of hair
    Clasps my wrist, and if I should fall,
This to my maid I pray you bear—
    This to my maid, comrade—that is all !"
    *   *   *   *   *
There is no moon, but the sky is fair—
    The sky is fair, though the stars be few.
In the shadow of Death he is lying there :
    In the shadow of Death, at twenty-two !

His pulse is still, and his wrist is bare.
    Clasp of gold with its sunny braid
The slender wrist of a maid shall wear—
    The slender wrist of his peerless maid !

ONLY ONE.

"THERE is no cloud in all the sky:
    I hear the distant bugles play:
You tremble, sister! so do I—
    Our soldiers both come home to-day."

"One cloud there is, Maud, on the blue:
    'Tis but a rustic horn you hear:
I tremble? Nay! Or, if I do,
    It is not for myself I fear."

"Not for yourself! For whom then, pray?
    For whom can you have cause to feel?—
Those are the bugles, Anne, I say,
    And—ah! I see the flash of steel!"

The sabres glitter in the sun:
    The war-worn ranks ride slowly past:
One soldier halts—ah! only one!—
    And cries, "At last, beloved, at last!"

His steed stands, wistful-eyed, apart,
  And looks upon the ripening grain;
But who is to the rider's heart
  Thus pressed, again and yet again?

Alas! one cloud still spans the sky,
  And still the distant bugles play!
Poor Maud! the ranks have long passed by;
  But only one came home to-day!

PROTO-MARTYR NOSTER.

HE wore nor crown nor purple; held no state
   Hedged by the spectre of the " Right Divine "
That haunts the visions of a kingly line:
He was his People's Chieftain, and their mate!
Chosen from their midst as meet to bear the weight
Of office worthily; ay, more! approved
By sorest trial steadfast to the trust
His worth had won! To save the land he loved,
Amid the storm of strife, the heat of lust,
And envy's gloom, and faction's blinding dust,
He kept the unflinching tenor of his path
Toward its bright zenith—till the Archfiend's spite
Belched, hot from hell, a minion of his wrath,
With one fell blow to plunge a world in night!

   April 15, 1865.

VAGARIES.

HOW WINTER COMETH.

HE comes! The tardy Winter comes!
  I hear his footsteps through the Nights!
  I hear his vanguard from the heights
March through the pines with muffled drums!

His naked feet are on the mead:
  The grass-blades stiffen in his path:
  No tear for child of Earth he hath;
No pity for her tender seed!

The bare oaks shudder at his breath:
  A moment by the stream he stays—
  Its melody is mute! A glaze
Creeps o'er its dimples, as of death!

From fettered stream and blackened moor,
  The city's walls he, silent, nears:
  The mansions of the Rich he fears!
He storms the cabins of the Poor!

3

The curtained couch—the glowing hearth—
  The frost-rimed Greybeard's power defy:
  He curses as he hurries by—
And strikes the Beggar, dead, to Earth!

For every gleaming hall he spares,
  A hundred hearthless hovels hold
  Hearts pulseless, crisp with ice, and cold,
Watched by a hundred grim Despairs!

The forests grow by His command
  Who saith, "He lendeth to the Lord
  Who giveth to the Poor!" Your hoard
Is His! Ye—stewards of the land!

Here is your Mission! Ye who feed
  Your lavish fires! Not afar,
  But at your doors, your Heathen are!
God's Poor—your creditors! Take heed!

The path is long to Pagan shores:
  Their skies are sunny: God o'er all!
  The Winter's deadly harvests fall
Around you! Deal your Master's stores!

HOW SPRING COMETH.

MARK where she comes—the hoyden Spring!
　　Her nascent bosom swelling fast,
　Her fresh lips parting to the blast,
And all her beauties blossoming!

She wantons with the regal Sun,
　　And bids the inconstant god caress
　　The very turf her wild feet press,
The humblest shrub she breathes upon.

The slumberous draperies that close
　　Around the palaces of Earth,
　　Flap—startled by her passing mirth—
And fall! She tarries not for those!

But from the squalid window-sill
　　She sweeps the scanty veil aside
　　And enters, radiant as a bride—
The sun-kiss hovering round her still!

Like music here her laughter falls;
　And echoes—as of Summer bees,
　And bird-songs through soft-swaying trees—
Seem quivering on the naked walls!

Echoes too often false as fair!
　So far from actual sense they seem,
　The listener holds them as a dream
Whose waking hath no promise there!

Ye microscopic souls, that cling
　To such small specks of spirit-light
　That all beyond your reach is night;—
Ye, bigots!—rob the Poor of Spring!

Ye bar them from the fresh free sod!
　To these wan children of the soil
　Ye make the Sabbath-Rest a toil—
A dungeon of the house of God!

Fling wide your sombre gates, and bid
　These weary workers forth, to share
　Life's heritage of spring-tide! There
The secret of God's Rest is hid!

STORM AND SUN.

"YOU think there will be a storm," you say?
So do I!
In my soul it hath lowered all day! All day,
A canopy, storm-glutted, sullen, and gray,
But cloven at times by the lightning's play,
Hath hung o'er my spirit-sky!

"O! you only spoke of the gathering gloom
Overhead?"
Ay! a ripple of rain-drops, a flash, a boom!—
And the sun-gold again in your curtained room,
And the air all steeped in a misty perfume
From the grateful earth-throats shed!

But I—I speak of a deadlier cloud—
Do you heed?
Its thunders mayhap will not be so loud,
But its bolt will strike!—and a crimsoned shroud
May reek in its track! Is your hard heart cowed?
Dare you taunt me to the deed?

Ha! ha! Do you think I have not seen?
    If he creep
But once more, my heart and its sunlight between—
My heart and its sunlight; you know what I mean—
The sod that he tramples shall not be green
    With all the tears you can weep!
      *   *   *   *

The storm came, and found us silent—and sped!
    Then, she spake:
"Love is not all woven of one bright thread;
There is steel with its gold, you have often said:
I *was* hard! And you? Let it pass! Overhead
    All is gold! Will not *your* sun break?"

CATALPA.

THE South-wind in sensuous kisses
  Sweeps warm o'er my humid lips,
And wanders with amorous touches
Through my hair, like an airy wanton
  With invisible finger-tips.

I lie in the purple clover,
  And over my languid head
The Catalpa's proud-lipped flowers
In a white and purple splendour
  Their fragrant incense shed.

I lie breast-deep in the clover,
  While the broad Catalpa-leaves
With a slumberous swaying lull me,
Like the soft seductive dream-spell
  That the Eastern Houri weaves.

I lie and dream of a Summer
  All flushed with the sensuous glow

Of a love that swept like the South-wind
Over every chord of passion—
   A Summer, ah! long ago!

I dream of the amorous fingers
   Of one who was not of air;
And I thrill with a nameless rapture
As her hand's electric velvet
   Threads the tangles of my hair.

I dream of a humid fragrance
   More warm than the South-wind's kiss;
More sweet than the sweetest flowers;
And lips upon lips lie folded
   In a lingering dream of bliss.

I dream of a murmur softer
   Than the whisper of Houri spell;
And through its delicious music
The echoes of two souls' passion
   In ravishing accents swell.

     *   *   *   *

Alas! for the South-wind faileth;
   Alas! for the broad leaves rest;

Alas! for the proud-lipped flowers
Are shrunken, and from the clover
  The purple hath gone to the West.

Alas! for the warm caresses!
  Alas! for the passion-glow!
And alas! for the love's soft music
That I heard in the swaying Catalpa,
  Of a Summer long ago!
    3*

THE SECRET OF THE ASPEN.

A CLOUD hangs over the morning
    This drear Autumnal day,
And the robins that sang on the Aspen
    Have shivered, and flown away.

The Aspen itself is leafless,
    Save the topmost spray; but there,
Two last withered leaves are trembling,
    Though there is not a breath of air.

A weird old tree is that Aspen;
    A low-voiced wizard—a seer—
In whose solemn, quaint unquiet,
    A secret of life is clear.

Through the fevered flush of summer,
    When the stillness is zenith-deep,
And within the slumbering forests
    The winds have nestled to sleep;—

That Aspen alone is restless,
  And trembles in fitful starts,
Like the guilty, when memory's poignard
  Pricks the canker in their hearts.

And to-day, those two leaves, lonely
  And sear, on its topmost spray,
Seem like two souls, fluttering faintly
  To pass from their shrunken clay :—

Two souls that, in life's fair Spring-tide,
  Climbed nearest its golden zone,
To wither thus in life's Autumn,
  On its bleakest summit—alone !

Yes, a weird old tree is that Aspen !
  A low-voiced wizard—a seer !
And he who will sit in its shadow,
  This secret of life may hear :—

Through its solemn, quaint unquiet,
  A wondrous whisper comes,
Like the murmur of bees in clover,
  Or an echo of far-off drums :—

And he who lists, when the shadows
    Are creeping, like ghosts, from the West,
May hear :—"Since the doom of Adam,
    The Soul's one curse is Unrest!"

THE GLOVE-KISS.

.

BELLE kissed me! Did she kiss me?
 Ah, no! I slumbered still!
Rests there a sleeping shadow where
 The sun-rays kiss the hill?

Belle kissed me! Did she kiss me?
 Ah, no! My brow ne'er flushed!
Pales still the longing fruit, o'er which
 The Summer noon hath gushed?

Sly Belle! Thou didst not kiss me!
 Else would this heart of mine
Thrill yet, as when the sensuous lip
 Is moist with royal wine.

So thus, coy Belle, *I* kiss *thee*,
 And still the gloves are thine!
" More blest to give than to receive "—
 The precept is divine!

LATAKEA.

SITTING alo'ne in my room;
Smoking Latakea;
Suddenly comes—an Idea,
Fluttering in through the gloom :—
Fluttering—muttering—strange fancies uttering—
Floats this Idea through the gloom.

" Fancy yourself a wreath
Of that Latakea,"—
Whispers the floating Idea—
" Wavering out on the breath :
Wavering—quavering—figureless, save a ring
Swept out of curl by a breath !

" Open your window, and see
How the wreath will sail
Eagerly out to the gale;
Vaporing forth, to be free :
Vaporing—tapering coyly—then capering
Madly, with joy to be free !

" Short-lived folly, oh Wreath!
  Headstrong Latakea!"—
  Mutters the cynic Idea—
" Venturing in the wind's teeth!
Venturing bent your ring—finally sent your ring
  Out-streaming, broken, to death!

" So with the smoker, youth!
  Merely wreath and ring!
  Out into life you fling;
Blundering on after Truth:
Blundering—wondering—while the Storm's sundering
  All of your life, save the ruth!"

Thus, all alone in my room,
  Smoking Latakea,
  Tauntingly came this Idea,
Fluttering in through the gloom:
Fluttering—muttering—these fancies uttering—
  Swept the Idea through the gloom!

DOGWOOD LEAVES.

I.

LOOK, Helen, the Autumn is young! As yet,
No gold in her kirtle of green she weaves:
But mark, ere her earliest sun is set,
How the red blood glows in the dogwood leaves!

II.

We plucked the dogwood blossoms, you know,—
The odorous blossoms of white and gold—
Together, one Spring-time, long ago.
Not long? O! yes! You have grown so old!

III.

So old? It was only this Spring, you say?
Nay! your heart is calm and your hand is cold;
Was it thus—did you turn your head away
When we gathered the blossoms of white and gold?

IV.

No! those were Spring-Mornings of Faith! You said:—
"Love doubts not, nor reasons; love believes!"
Now—alas! where the blossoms their odors spread,
There are only the blood-red dogwood leaves!

EPHEMERA.

I HEARD these words as I passed him :—
" The River of Life," quoth he :
He was old, and he spake as in terror ;
For, if he had sailed down that River,
  His shallop was near the sea !

But I, in my heart replying
  To the words this old man said,
I cried : " He speaketh a folly
Who likens Life to a River !"
  He halted, and turned his head.

I cried ; " Life is *not* a River !
  For the River ebbs and flows ;
And the leaf that it floated seaward
At morn,—lo ! the flood-tide flingeth
  On the flower-bank whence it rose !"

" What waif of Life, that hath floated
  To the Gulf without a name,

From the margin of Time,—Old Greybeard—
Met ever a wave returning,
　　To render it whence it came?"

But the old man smiled, as he trembled,
　And—"The River of Life"—he said,
And lifted his withered finger
And pointed, where, into the ocean
　The sunset heaven still bled;

And it seemed as a thirst and a terror
　Were at strife in this old man's soul;
And he murmured: "The waves of that River
Are the flood that, forever backward,
　The waifs of this Life shall roll!"

EPHEMERA

A WREN-PAIR built under my winaow;—
He sang, while she raised her brood:
At first they were shy; but after,
They daintily gathered the morsels
  I sat by the lintel and strewed.

Then the little ones, too, came bravely,
  And trustfully picked their fill,
And chirruped a fearless chorus
To the elder's grateful allegro
  From my very window-sill.

"You are going," I said to Inez:
  "You have learned to trust me, I know;—
And to love?"—"I *have* learned to love you!"
"Both will fade, ere another Summer,
  As words that are writ on snow!"

She laughed—she frowned; "You are cruel!
  My whole heart's pages shall show

These past Summer lessons, forever!"
The wrens, too, went with that Summer:
  I sighed, and bade Inez go!

A wren-pair sought under my window
  Their nest, in the olden spot:
I sprinkled crumbs on the lintel;
But the birds were as shy as strangers,
  And the Summer lessons—forgot!

I watched, with an anxious patience,
  And hoped, with a nameless pain,
For the fearless faith's renewal;
But the olden Summer lessons
  Had all to be learned again!

Yet the wrens will sing on my lintel
  With the olden trust, I know:
While the Summer lessons, written
On those heart-pages of Inez,
  Are as words that were writ on snow!

FROM ALPHA TO OMEGA.

OVER THE SNOW.

OVER the frozen highway;—
　　Gleaming with crystalline light;—
Hiding the skeleton-furrows
　　In a velvet robe of white;—

Seemingly slumber inviting,
　　Stainless, unruffled, serene;—
Thus lay the snow for my journey
　　Omega and Alpha between!

Out from the sun-girt Alpha;—
　　Forth o'er the glittering crust;—
Leaving firm foot-prints behind me;—
　　On to Omega—and Dust!

Saying—"O! deep-pressed foot-prints!
　　Henceforth, not looking in vain,
Often from restful Omega
　　My heart-gaze shall see you again!"

" Many will mark you, who love me:
  Where I have stumbled, will leap;
Where I have slumbered, will hasten ;
  Where I have fallen, will weep!"

Foolishest folly of follies!
  Still in the shadows afar
Lurketh the restful Omega!
  Vanished the foot-prints are!

Vanished the snow, and the foot-prints!
  Rugged and furrowed the crust!
Over the highway I struggle
  Still, to Omega—and Dust!

THE FEAST-NIGHT OF THE TWO QUEENS.

I.

LAST night was a Queen's Feast-night!
 The Queen of the timid stars
That tremble in legions of scintillant light
 Around the red pennon of Mars!

II.

Yes! last night the Moon-Queen won
 Her maidenhood's richest prime;
And her radiant face snatched a kiss from the Sun,
 To illumine the night-march of Time.

I.

Last night was a Queen's Feast-night!
 The Queen of my Life—my Love!
The planet that thrills me with throbbing delight,
 As the Moon thrills the ether above.

II.

Yes! last night my Heart-Queen won
 Her maidenhood's furthest goal;
And her kisses still glow, like a central Sun,
 Through the innermost night of my soul!

THE MESSENGER-YEARS.

O F lines to the years that fly,
　　And lines to the years that are born,
　There are pages on pages!
But the clouds in each sunset sky,
And the clouds in each sky of morn,
Have never seemed twice the same, men say,
　Through all the past ages.

Then why should I stifle the song
That wells from my heart to my lips,
　Of the Flying, and the Coming?
The Two Years shadows are long;
And many may sit in eclipse,
Whose darkened hearts will be glad, perchance,
　To list to my humming.

Why do ye sad tears shed,
With your dim eyes backward bent
　On the Year that is reckoned?
Let your Dead bury their Dead!
Years are but Messengers, sent

Forward from God to man : they return
    When the Great Hand has beckoned !

  Is it the fault of the Sage,
  If his counsel be spurned by the herd
    For the mountebank's leer ?
  Scourge ye your Master's Page,
  If ye hear, and yet heed not the word
That he brings from His awful lips, and breathes
    In your obdurate ear ?

  No ! If the errand be sped,
  And the Messenger-Year flit back
    To the halls of the Past ;—
  Let your Dead bury their Dead !
  Pause not to weep on their track !
He that hath slept, be it never so long,
    Shall waken at last !

  Waken, then, ye that have slept !
  List not the echoes of THEN—
    They are fathomless air !
  If through past shadows ye crept ;
  Spring toward the sunshine like men !
Leap to the promise of Now, and hail
    A new Messenger there !
  4

THE KITE.

UPLIFTED in the invisible palms
    Of the strong North Wind,
It seeks the clear, celestial calms
.   That bask, sun-trancèd, in the Upper Space;
    But still regards with mournful face
      The Earth it leaves behind.

Anon, made drunken by the abyss
    Of the giddy height,
It courts the clouds with wanton kiss,
    And, reeling, thinks amid the stars to sing,
    Forgetful of the sordid string
      That rules its span of flight.

But lo! a "messenger" is sped
    Up the murmuring cord!
This fluttering waif—this paper shred—
    Sufficeth for a token of the bond
    That saith: "Thou mayst not soar beyond
      Will of thine Urchin Lord!"

Thus, in the invisible palms of Thought
    My Spirit is borne
Where glimpses of the Light are caught,
  And, drunken with the ecstasy of flight,
  Spreads eager pinions from the Night
    Unto Empyrean Morn. ,

With closed eyes hither turned, it flies
    Upon wanton wing
Through clouds where Memory lurking lies—
  Beyond the troubled Present's Middle Space—
  Zenithward still ; nor feels its race
    Checked by Earth's sordid string.

But lo ! along the chord of Life
    There passeth a thrill :
A pang—a sense of breathing strife—
  Are token of the inexorable bond
  That saith :—" Thou mayst not soar beyond
    Thy Despot-Body's will !"

THE TWO SHADOWS.

IT was a frolic-morn in May:
   The world looked young and very fair,
  That morn, to us: 'Tis now—O, Claire!—
How long ago I dare not say!

Our hearts were very full of mirth:
   We thought that Life could never pall:
   We sate beneath the garden wall,
In love with every thing on earth!

The Years, we thought, were all our own.
   Claire gaily snatched away her hand;
   Then bade me, "on my peril, stand!"
And sketched my shadow on the stone.

It was a profile round and fair:
   No angles marred its lines of youth:
   We laughed; and then, with feebler truth,
I sketched the glorious face of Claire.

   *   *   *   *

A Life! O God! how mere a speck—
  A microscopic shallop—tossed
  On the vast waves of Time, and lost!
Too frail to leave a trace of wreck!

The Years we counted cycles, flown!
  My shadow now, sharp edged as care!
  And not a trace, on earth, of Claire,
Save on my heart, and that cold stone!

THE SNOW.

A FANTASY.

HOW it snows!
　　Through the blackness of Night,
How silent—how white
Drop the trembling flakes! What a luminous light
　　Upward glows
From the breast of the snows!
From the pulseless, untrodden breast of the snows!

　　One soft sigh
Floating out on the air
From an infant at prayer,
If it met with an errant snow-flake there,
　　This would die!
This would melt in the sigh—
Would dissolve to a tear, in that infantine sigh!

　　Yet the gale
With its bitterest blast
Through the snow-flakes has passed;

And lo! they are sunk to their slumber at last,
    In the vale,
    In spite of the gale!
Still virgin, unmolten, in spite of the gale!

    So the Soul!—
    If it wander astray
    Through the errors of clay,
And meet with a treacherous breath, on its way
    To its goal:—
    This shall melt the lost Soul!
Though never so feeble—shall melt the lost Soul!

    So the Soul!—
    Through the fierce blasts of Care;—
    Through the nights of Despair;—
If the faith in its mission and Master be there;—
    To the goal
    Will attain the pure Soul!
Will, in triumph eternal, attain the pure Soul!

THE LAMP.

'TWAS written—"Absence conquers Love!"
    Forsooth, fond fools, go weep!
A blindfold vigil well may prove
    A weary thing to keep!

But Friendship is an Anchorite,
    Whose ever wakeful eye
Turns, hope-illumined, toward the light,
    And marks the days go by.

And Friendship's vestal lamp will burn
    Within its lonely fane,
Till its far Priestess shall return
    To give it oil again!

But ah! should she, for other shrines,
    Forget the distant spark;—
The lonely lamp no longer shines:
    The silent fane grows dark!

Not Absence, then, nor verge of space,
  Alone, dims Friendship's glow;
But Silence, with averted face,
  May let the lamp burn low!
   4*

IN THE PAVILION.

LIKE slender serpents, quaintly coiled and golden,
   Along the path lie strewn the chestnut-blooms,
Even to the portal, moss-begirt and moulden,
    In forest glooms.

Through vaulted chestnut-boughs, dark-leaved and solemn,
   The full-orbed glances of the sunset wind,
In crimson threads, around each crumbling column
    With ivy twined.

A sentinel crow, guarding his comrades' pillage,
   From a tall oak his warning discord flings,
And ever and anon from some far village
    The vesper rings.

How long since, in that wood-embayed Pavilion,
   Hand-clasped they sate, and hymned the eternal song
With one refrain—" My love! my own! my Lilian!"
    Ay, heart, how long?

The chestnut-blooms that fell in golden mazes
   That halcyon summer, now in ashen mould
Lie withered, as the heart of him who gazes,
      Calm-pulsed, and cold!

Only one summer, say'st thou? Fool! Whole ages
   Have heaped the sear leaves of dead passion-flowers
Upon life's garden, since those gilded pages
      Marked its soft hours.

Sit with me here, Pet; let me whisper "Lilian—
   My Lilian!" Pshaw! I crave your pardon, Sweet;
There's a strange echo in this old Pavilion
      That will repeat!

Come, fair Caprice! see! yonder shadow flitting
   Through the gray wood, Kate, is the Bird of Night:
Let us go in; that laugh is more befitting
      A scene of light!

REST.

I.

HE walked upon the silent shore,
  And marked the restful billows roll,
And heard the song their surges bore,
Whose burden evermore
  Found siren echoes in his soul.
" Life is not worth its woe," they said;
" But Rest is with the Dead—the Dead!"

II.

Athwart the slowly dying Day—
  Above the slowly swaying sea—
On the horizon, far away,
A luminous castle lay,
  With crimson banners floating free,
In bar and blazon manifold,
Across the sunset fields of gold.

III.

" O! tristful truth! O! lustrous lie!"
  From out his struggling spirit came

Unsought, this double-tongued reply:
He looked upon the sky
  Whence flashed the castle's oriflame,
And murmured, " Would my soul were free!
Is not *there* Rest, O! siren Sea?"

IV.

The golden glories faded fast
  From crumbling tower and battlement:
A pall, funereal, ashen, vast,
O'er all the west was cast:
  The banners from the walls were rent:
And still the siren surges said:—
"Ay! Rest is with the Dead—the Dead!"

V.

Then all was darkness for a space:
  He stood upon the verge of Doom!
Alas! no mortal eye might trace
The horror in his face.
  He heard the sullen surges boom,
And bent his brow above the brine,
And moaned, " Thy Rest, O Sea! be mine!'

VI.

But sweetly—even as he spoke,
   And stretched his longing arms afar—
Close to his ear a whisper woke;
And on the Night there broke
   The splendor of the Evening Star!
Warm lips to his cold lips were pressed,
That sighed :—" Ungrateful ! Love is Rest !"

AU REVOIR.

I.

'TWAS but a year ago to-day!
  We drank love then, as revellers wine:
Love was our life, we used to say:
  I quaffed from your lips, you from mine.

II.

The parting hour struck like a knell:
  The dark ship seemed a funeral car:
I strove in vain to say—Farewell!
  Your lips closed mine with—AU REVOIR!

III.

To those two words of hope I clung
  As clings a wrecked one to the spar:
Forgive me, for my heart was young,
  And youth trusts woman's " *au revoir.*"

IV.

Last night we met again—we two,
  Alone! . . . None save the stars may tell
How yields the old love to the new,
  And " *Au Revoir*" becomes " FAREWELL!"

THE TREASURE-SHIPS:

A FRAGMENT.

THE Master looked across the sea:
　"Lo! where the ships come back to me!

"Treasure of Southern isles they bring,
And sweet-voiced Southern maids, that sing!

"Rare maidens, in whose liquid eyes
An ocean, mooned by Love, there lies!

"Ho! ho! the Greybeard drank the wine,
And all these treasure-ships are mine!"

Again he looked across the sea:
"Blow, South wind! blow my maids to me!"

The South wind blew across the sea:
The breakers laughed in devilish glee.

The surf-steeds tossed their hoary mane:
He looked across the sea again.

The moon-rays, through a broken cloud,
Fell on a Dead Man in his shroud!

Strange wrecks were dashed upon the shore:
The murderer saw his ships no more!

MA MIE:

A GASCONADE.

I.

AN April Rainbow, flecked with every hue
    Of sun and sky and sea,
Glowing through opals of coruscant dew:
    Thus through my heart's prism glows—Ma mie!

II.

A wild, warm wind, that, flushing through the vine
    Of sun-loved Gascony,
Thrills its pale juices with the blush of wine:
    Thus through my heart's blood thrills—Ma mie!

III.

A sigh down-borne with fragrance now, that stoops
    O'er some low balcony,
And its rich freight to some bared bosom droops:
    Thus to my bared heart droops—Ma mie!

IV.

Ay! she hath all these charms! And yet—and yet—
    Lost heart! Ah! woe is me!
The Arc is mist! The Gascon wind hath met
    The sigh, and—what is left—Ma mie?

SUA CULPA.

SHE sighed: He would not hear her sigh!
　　Up from the sun-disk, veined with gold,
Cloud-scymitars in blades of blood,
Like Fates flared o'er the ebbing flood :—
　　Flared out; and all the day was told!

She wept: He would not hear her weep!
　　The River still ebbed toward the sea;
And drunk with the treacherous anodynes
Of the odorous Summer jessamines,
　　His soul still slumbered fatally.

She prayed: He would not hear her prayer!
　　The Night-wind swept in fiery breaths
Like fever-flushes through his sleep:
There was no dew—though she did weep—
　　Fell on his spirit—not even Death's!

She left him! . . . Then, his soul awoke!
　　The storm came hurtling through the Night:
The angry River rushed roaring back,
Bearing strange Wrecks upon its track ;—
　　Strange? Ay! For one . . . was swathed in white!

TOO LATE!

A S, through the wind-waved mist of morning,
Down a far sweep of sylvan glade
Come glimpses of some glistening statue,
Perplexed with shifting sheen and shade ;—

So, through a veil of spectral vapors,
Now shrined in sun, now steeped in gloom,
I see a sweet, mysterious phantom
Of one beloved beyond the tomb.

" To love, and then to lose, is better
Than never to have loved?" Ah, well!
But of a love by loss engendered—
A phœnix-passion—who may tell?

Think that I never loved her, living!
Think of the awful throe of birth—
The sudden travail of my passion—
Begun the night she quitted earth!

And ever since, beyond forgetting
  Of wasting care or wild caprice,
It grows upon me in the pauses,
  And feeds upon its own increase.

And ever, in the spectral shadows,
  Now sun-enshrined, now draped in gloom,
I see the sad, mysterious phantom
  Of her beloved beyond the tomb!

CLAIRE:

A SPIRIT-MEMORY.

CLAIRE was my Soul-Twin!
　　One-hearted—
O'er her tomb we were Death-wed,
　　Not parted!
Claire was my Soul-Twin—
　　My Bride!

The Sun-rays that nestled
　　Among the gold floss
　　Of her hair ;—
The passionate Winds that wrestled
　　The fragrance to share
　　That distilled from her hair—
　　Ay! were wanton to share
The incense that breathed
From invisible censers that swayed through her hair,
　　And floated and wreathed
　　Round the aureous hair

Of my Sun-caressed Claire ;—
Oh ! I envied them, cursed them !
With mad hand dispersed them !

But, ah ! vainly,
         Insanely,
Alas ! thus I strove
To avert Heaven's love
         From my Bride !
The Angels grew jealous,
And so—it befell us,
         She died !

Oh ! God ! in the horror
Of impious sorrow
I cursed Thee, denied Thee,
Reviled Thee, defied Thee !

Oh ! God ! I repent me !
   Contritely, bitterly,
Prostrate before Thee,
   Abjectly, utterly,
I thank Thee, adore Thee,
For this Thou hast sent me !

My Darling is dead!
But I hold
One floss-curl of gold
Of her hair,
And the fragrance of old
Still is shed
To my prayer!
The ravishing incense still breathes through its gold,
As of old,
From invisible censers Thy Bounty hath fed;
Floating down through the air
From the luminous zone
Of Thy Throne–
From the brow of Thy Claire!
From the radiant brow of Thy Claire,
Shrinèd there!

UMBRA:

A HALF-SUNG SONG.

I AM singing in the sunshine:
  You are sighing in the shade:
Wherefore sigh when I am singing?
  "Shadow is of sunshine made."

Cynic! Answer! What are shadows,
  But the fleeting ghosts of Light?
Night is cradle of the Morning:
  "Rather Morn the tomb of Night."

Nay, then, I will change my measure:
  Faith is night, and Hope is morn:
Noon is Love: behold the zenith!—
  "Child! I was not eagle-born."

No! but born of woman, surely.
  What am I? O! look, and find,
In my eyes, Love's noon-tide blazing!—
  "Haply! Love has long been blind."

Cruel, cruel! Say, blasphemer,
  By what altar do you pray
That is never sun-illumined?—
  "Peace! By that of Yesterday!"

5

NEVER AGAIN.

GIVE o'er, give o'er! my heart is sore!
  Its aching chords your accents strain!
In vain you prate of manhood's force;
In vain strew maxims on my course;
My heart is pulseless to their plea:
  They rouse no echoes in my brain:
It seems to me—it seems to me
  That I can never smile again!

When passion rolls o'er human souls,
  Past woes assuage not present pain.
What are the olden memories worth?
Dead ashes, on a blazing hearth!
The actual flame burns fierce and free;
  Winds stir the ashen Past in vain:
It seems to me—it seems to me
  That I can never smile again!

What do I care if one despair
  Hath swept, as sweeps the autumn rain,

O'er some dimmed landscape of my life?
Still bleeds beneath the bravo's knife—
Who stabs and stabs, with sateless glee—
    At each fresh wound a severed vein:
It seems to me—it seems to me
    That I can never smile again!

Experience? A thing of sense!
    An unctuous barber of the brain,
Who dresses it with studied care,
And smooths it here, and oils it there:
You strive, within the heart's Dead Sea,
    To sink life's bitter fruits, in vain!
It seems to me—it seems to me
    That I shall never smile again!

THE AUTUMN LEAVES.

STILL in spectral crowds the misty clouds
 Drive past, though the moon is clear;
Like the hurried flight of a host by night,
O'er a wintry plain where the tents gleam white,
 And the silence strains the ear.

Ay! the moon is clear, and the restless stars
 Are shaking their diamond crowns:
Yet the forests wail, and the voice of the gale
Is sharp with the rattle of leaves, that sail,
 Like witches, over the downs.

Skurrying over the fields they go—
 Withered, and shrunken, and wan—
In the elfin wrack of the Night-wind's track:
O, they are merry! When Spring comes back,
 Look for them! Where have they gone?

Where have they gone? In the rosy morn
 Of a day not long gone by,

They drank the dew of a life all new,
And sported with every breeze that blew,
  As if Summer ne'er would die.

Where have they gone? Dance on, O! leaves,
  While the Autumn wind endures!
Be he gentle or clown who treads you down,
In the furrowed field or the silken town,
  Let him read his life in yours!

GONE:

A NEW-YEAR'S MONODY.

I.

AS the snow-flake on the sea;—
   As the dew-drop on the lawn;—
As the frost-rime on the tree;—
   There, and gone! Here, and gone!
So hath passed a Year to me.

II.

As the sunrise on the sea;—
   As the violet on the lawn;—
As the spring-bud on the tree;—
   Flushed of morn! Promise-born!
So is born a Year to me.

III.

When this vanished Year began,
   Looking seaward and to shore,

Thus my pilgrim-ditty ran,
  O'er and o'er, once before,
From Life's " Beersheba to Dan!"

IV.

Pilgrimage of self-deceit!
  Angel-thwarted, Demon-ruled,
Here I stand with weary feet;—
  Promise-fooled, sorrow-schooled;—
Where the Past and Future meet!

V.

Here I halt, and fling my staff
  Scornfully beside the way.
Here I sit me down and laugh,
  As I say: "Come what may,
Cup of care no more I quaff!

VI.

" PAST! I drink, in Lethean wine,
  To thy memories of pain!
Fond and foolish tear of mine
  Ne'er again shalt thou drain:
I have done with thee and thine!

VII.

" FUTURE ! At thy phantom-feast
  I'll no more play Barmecide !
PRESENT ! *Thou* art mine, at least !
  Let me ride on thy tide,
While Life's sun still gilds the East !"

THE END.